Coffee vending machine for Business

Ever Wondered How a Coffee Vending Machine Can Skyrocket Your Workplace Productivity?

Content

23. Investing in research and development

24. Keeping up with industry trends

25. Expanding your business to new locations

26. Building brand awareness

27. Offering promotions and discounts

28. Implementing customer feedback

29. Evaluating business performance

30. Improving customer service

31. Establishing a training program for employees

32. Upgrading coffee vending machines

33. Building a company culture

34. Developing a crisis management plan

35. Managing risks and challenges

36. Staying current with industry news

37. Offering additional products and services

38. Establishing a presence on social media

39. Building relationships with customers

40. Preparing for growth and success.

Introduction

Introduction to Coffee Vending Machines

Welcome to the world of coffee vending machines! Whether you're an entrepreneur looking to start a new business or just interested in learning more about these machines, you've come to the right place. Coffee vending machines are a convenient and efficient way to provide people with a quick and easy cup of coffee. In this chapter, we'll take a closer look at what coffee vending machines are, how they work, and why they're so popular.

What are Coffee Vending Machines?

Coffee vending machines are automated machines that dispense hot drinks, including coffee. They come in various sizes, styles, and capacities, but the basic concept is the same: to provide customers with a quick and easy way to get their coffee fix. Some coffee vending machines can dispense just a simple cup of coffee, while others are more advanced and can make a variety of drinks, including espresso, cappuccino, and latte.

How do Coffee Vending Machines Work?

Coffee vending machines work by grinding coffee beans, brewing the coffee, and dispensing it into a cup. The process starts when you insert money or a credit card into the machine. Next, you select the type of drink you want. Some machines have buttons that let you choose from a variety of drinks, while others have a touch screen that guides you through the process. After you've made your selection, the machine grinds the coffee beans, brews the coffee, and dispenses it into a cup.

Why are Coffee Vending Machines Popular?

Coffee vending machines are popular for several reasons. First, they're convenient. People can get their coffee quickly and easily without having to wait in line at a coffee shop. Second, they're efficient. Coffee vending machines can make a variety of drinks, so customers can get exactly what they want without having to go to a coffee shop. Third, they're cost-effective. Coffee vending machines can be less expensive than coffee shops, so people can get a cup of coffee for a lower price.

In conclusion, coffee vending machines are a great way to provide people with a quick and easy cup of coffee. They're convenient, efficient, and cost-effective, which is why they're so popular. Whether you're an entrepreneur looking to start a new business or just interested in learning more about these machines, we hope you've found this chapter helpful.

Understanding the Market for Coffee Vending Machines

As you dive into the world of coffee vending machines, it's important to understand the market you'll be entering. This chapter will explore the current state of the coffee vending machine market, including trends, competition, and opportunities for growth. By understanding the market, you'll be better equipped to make informed decisions about your coffee vending machine business.

Market Size and Growth

The coffee vending machine market has been growing steadily over the past few years and is expected to continue growing in the coming years. According to recent market research, the global coffee vending machine market was valued at $3.1 billion in 2020 and is expected to reach $4.3 billion by 2026, growing at a compound annual growth rate (CAGR) of 4.7% during the forecast period. This growth is driven by the increasing demand for convenient and efficient coffee options, as well as the growth of the food and beverage industry.

Market Trends

There are several trends shaping the coffee vending machine market. One trend is the increasing demand for high-quality coffee. People are willing to pay more for a better cup of coffee, and coffee vending machines are offering just that. Another trend is the growth of technology. Coffee vending machines are becoming more advanced, offering features like touch screens, Wi-Fi connectivity, and more. Finally, there's a trend towards eco-friendliness. Coffee vending machines are becoming more environmentally friendly, using biodegradable and recyclable materials.

Competition

There is significant competition in the coffee vending machine market. There are several large players, as well as many small, local businesses. Some of the major players in the market include Nestle, Mars, and Coca-Cola. To stand out in this competitive market, it's important to offer a high-quality product, provide excellent customer service, and differentiate yourself from your competitors.

Opportunities for Growth

There are several opportunities for growth in the coffee vending machine market. One opportunity is to expand into new markets, such as offices, schools, and hospitals. Another opportunity is to offer additional products and services, such as snacks, cold drinks, and more. Finally, there's an opportunity to invest in research and development, developing new and innovative coffee vending machines that meet the needs of customers.

In conclusion, the coffee vending machine market is growing and offers opportunities for growth. By understanding the market trends, competition, and opportunities for growth, you'll be better equipped to succeed in the coffee vending machine business. Whether you're an entrepreneur starting a new business or an established business looking to grow, we hope this chapter has been helpful.

Choosing the Right Coffee Vending Machine for Your Business

When it comes to starting a coffee vending machine business, one of the most important decisions you'll make is choosing the right machine. With so many options on the market, it can be overwhelming to know where to start. In this chapter, we'll explore the factors you should consider when choosing a coffee vending machine for your business, so you can make an informed decision.

Consider Your Business Needs

The first factor to consider when choosing a coffee vending machine is your business needs. What type of business are you running? How many customers will you be serving? What type of coffee do you want to offer? These are all important questions to answer before making a decision. For example, if you're running a small office, you may only need a small machine that can dispense a few cups of coffee at a time. On the other hand, if you're running a busy coffee shop, you may need a larger machine that can dispense a variety of drinks.

Consider Your Budget

The second factor to consider when choosing a coffee vending machine is your budget. Coffee vending machines can range in price from a few hundred dollars to tens of thousands of dollars. It's important to determine how much you're willing to spend before making a decision. Keep in mind that the most expensive machines are not always the best choice. It's important to choose a machine that meets your business needs and fits within your budget.

Consider the Features

The third factor to consider when choosing a coffee vending machine is the features. What features do you need in a machine? Do you need a machine that can dispense a variety of drinks? Do you need a machine with a touch screen? Do you need a machine with Wi-Fi connectivity? These are all important questions to answer when choosing a coffee vending machine. Consider the features that are important to you and your business, and choose a machine that meets those needs.

Consider the Brand

The fourth factor to consider when choosing a coffee vending machine is the brand. There are many different brands on the market, and each brand offers different features and benefits. Consider the reputation of the brand and the support they offer. Do they have a good track record for reliability and customer service? These are important factors to consider when choosing a coffee vending machine.

Consider Your Location

The final factor to consider when choosing a coffee vending machine is your location. What type of environment will the machine be located in? Will it be located indoors or outdoors? Will it be located in a busy area or a quiet area? These are important questions to answer when choosing a coffee vending machine, as they can impact the type of machine you need and the features you require.

In conclusion, choosing the right coffee vending machine for your business requires careful consideration of several factors. Consider your business needs, budget, features, brand, and location when making a decision. By taking the time to consider these factors, you'll be able to choose the right machine for your business, ensuring success and customer satisfaction.

Factors to Consider When Selecting a Coffee Vending Machine

When it comes to starting a coffee vending machine business, choosing the right machine is essential. With so many options on the market, it's important to consider the factors that will affect your decision. In this chapter, we'll explore the key factors you should consider when selecting a coffee vending machine, so you can make an informed choice.

1. Capacity

The first factor to consider when selecting a coffee vending machine is the capacity. This refers to the number of cups of coffee the machine can dispense at one time. If you're running a small business, a machine with a smaller capacity may be sufficient. However, if you're running a busy coffee shop, you may need a machine with a larger capacity. Consider the number of customers you'll be serving and choose a machine that can meet your needs.

2. Speed

The second factor to consider when selecting a coffee vending machine is the speed. This refers to the time it takes for the machine to dispense a cup of coffee. If you're running a busy business, a machine with a fast dispensing time is essential. Consider the number of customers you'll be serving and choose a machine that can keep up with the demand.

3. Variety of Drinks

The third factor to consider when selecting a coffee vending machine is the variety of drinks the machine can dispense. Some machines only offer basic coffee, while others can dispense a range of drinks, such as espresso, cappuccino, and hot chocolate. Consider the type of business you're running and choose a machine that can dispense the drinks your customers want.

4. Maintenance and Upkeep

The fourth factor to consider when selecting a coffee vending machine is the maintenance and upkeep. This refers to the effort required to keep the machine running smoothly. Some machines require more maintenance than others. Consider the time and resources you have available for maintenance and choose a machine that fits within your budget and schedule.

5. Price

The fifth factor to consider when selecting a coffee vending machine is the price. Coffee vending machines can range in price from a few hundred dollars to tens of thousands of dollars. Consider your budget and choose a machine that fits within your price range. Keep in mind that the most expensive machines are not always the best choice. It's important to choose a machine that meets your business needs and fits within your budget.

6. Brand

The final factor to consider when selecting a coffee vending machine is the brand. There are many different brands on the market, and each brand offers different features and benefits.

Consider the reputation of the brand and the support they offer. Do they have a good track record for reliability and customer service? These are important factors to consider when choosing a coffee vending machine.

In conclusion, selecting the right coffee vending machine requires careful consideration of several factors. Consider the capacity, speed, variety of drinks, maintenance and upkeep, price, and brand when making a decision. By taking the time to consider these factors, you'll be able to choose a machine that meets your business needs, ensuring success and customer satisfaction.

Types of Coffee Vending Machines

When it comes to starting a coffee vending machine business, it's important to know the different types of machines available. Each type of machine offers unique features and benefits, and it's important to choose the right one for your business. In this chapter, we'll explore the different types of coffee vending machines, so you can make an informed choice.

1. Bean-to-Cup Coffee Machines

Bean-to-Cup coffee machines grind coffee beans to make each cup of coffee, providing a fresh and delicious cup every time. These machines are ideal for businesses that want to offer a high-quality coffee experience to their customers. They typically offer a range of drinks, including espresso, cappuccino, and latte.

2. Instant Coffee Machines

Instant coffee machines use pre-packaged coffee pods or packets to make each cup of coffee. These machines are easy to use and maintain, and they offer a convenient and cost-effective option for businesses that want to offer a variety of drinks. Instant coffee machines are typically the most affordable type of coffee vending machine.

3. Fresh Brew Coffee Machines

Fresh brew coffee machines use pre-ground coffee to make each cup of coffee. These machines are a good choice for businesses that want to offer a high-quality cup of coffee at an affordable price. Fresh brew coffee machines are typically less expensive than bean-to-cup machines and offer a variety of drinks.

4. Espresso Machines

Espresso machines are designed specifically to make espresso drinks. They offer a high-quality cup of coffee and are ideal for businesses that want to specialize in espresso-based drinks. Espresso machines can be expensive, but they are a good choice for businesses that want to offer a premium coffee experience to their customers.

5. Combo Machines

Combo machines are versatile machines that can dispense a variety of drinks, including coffee, tea, and hot chocolate. These machines are a good choice for businesses that want to offer a range of drinks to their customers. Combo machines can be more expensive than other types of coffee vending machines, but they offer the convenience of being able to dispense multiple drinks in one machine.

In conclusion, there are several different types of coffee vending machines available, each with unique features and benefits. Consider the type of business you're running and the type of drinks you want to offer when making a decision. By choosing the right type of machine, you'll be able to provide your customers with a high-quality coffee experience, ensuring success and customer satisfaction.

Coffee Vending Machine Features and Options

When choosing a coffee vending machine for your business, it's important to consider the features and options available. Different machines offer different features and options, and it's important to choose a machine that meets the needs of your business. In this chapter, we'll explore some of the common features and options available in coffee vending machines.

1. Drink Options

One of the most important features to consider is the number and type of drinks the machine can dispense. Different machines offer different drink options, so it's important to choose a machine that offers the drinks you want to serve. Some machines offer a range of drinks, including coffee, tea, and hot chocolate, while others specialize in espresso-based drinks.

2. Grinding Options

If you choose a bean-to-cup coffee machine, it's important to consider the grinding options available. Some machines have built-in grinders, while others use pre-ground coffee. Consider the type of coffee you want to serve and the level of control you want over the grinding process when making a decision.

3. Customization Options

Many coffee vending machines offer customization options, allowing you to adjust the strength and flavor of each cup of coffee. This is a great feature for businesses that want to offer a personalized experience to their customers. Consider the level of customization you want to offer when making a decision.

4. Payment Options

Consider the payment options available in the coffee vending machine you choose. Some machines accept coins, while others accept bills or credit cards. Consider the type of payment options you want to offer and the convenience you want to provide to your customers when making a decision.

5. Maintenance and Cleaning

Consider the maintenance and cleaning requirements of the coffee vending machine you choose. Some machines are easy to clean and maintain, while others require more time and effort. Consider the amount of time and resources you want to dedicate to maintenance and cleaning when making a decision.

6. Size and Capacity

Consider the size and capacity of the coffee vending machine you choose. Some machines are compact and ideal for small businesses, while others are larger and better suited for high-volume businesses. Consider the size of your business and the amount of space you have available when making a decision.

In conclusion, coffee vending machines offer a range of features and options. Consider the type of business you're running and the type of drinks you want to serve when making a decision. By choosing the right machine with the right features and options, you'll be able to provide your customers with a high-quality coffee experience, ensuring success and customer satisfaction.

Maintenance and Upkeep of Coffee Vending Machines

As with any piece of equipment, it's important to keep your coffee vending machine well-maintained in order to ensure it runs smoothly and provides high-quality drinks to your customers. In this chapter, we'll explore some of the key aspects of maintaining and keeping your coffee vending machine in good working order.

1. Regular Cleaning

Regular cleaning is one of the most important aspects of maintaining your coffee vending machine. Keeping your machine clean will not only improve the quality of the drinks it dispenses, but it will also help to prolong its lifespan. Most machines are equipped with self-cleaning functions, but it's still important to clean the machine manually on a regular basis, paying special attention to the brewing area and water tanks.

2. Replacing Consumables

Coffee vending machines use consumables such as coffee beans and water filters. Regularly replacing these consumables will ensure that the machine continues to dispense high-quality drinks. Some machines will let you know when it's time to replace a consumable, while others may require manual monitoring. Be sure to check the manufacturer's guidelines for recommendations on how often to replace consumables.

3. Regular Maintenance

Regular maintenance is an important aspect of keeping your coffee vending machine in good working order. This may involve checking and tightening screws, replacing worn or damaged parts, and cleaning the machine on a regular basis. Most manufacturers provide guidelines on the frequency of maintenance that is recommended for their machines. It's important to follow these guidelines in order to keep your machine running smoothly.

4. Servicing and Repairs

From time to time, your coffee vending machine may require servicing or repairs. This may be due to wear and tear or due to a malfunction. Regular servicing can help to identify potential problems before they become major issues. If your machine requires repairs, it's important to use a qualified repair professional to ensure that the machine is repaired correctly.

In conclusion, maintaining and keeping your coffee vending machine in good working order is crucial for ensuring its longevity and reliability. Regular cleaning, replacing consumables, performing regular maintenance, and having the machine serviced or repaired when necessary are all important aspects of keeping your machine in good condition. By taking good care of your machine, you'll be able to provide high-quality drinks to your customers, ensuring customer satisfaction and success for your business.

Setting up a Coffee Vending Machine Business

Are you looking to start your own coffee vending machine business? If so, this chapter is for you! In this chapter, we'll cover everything you need to know in order to successfully set up and operate a coffee vending machine business.

1. Conduct Market Research

Before starting any business, it's important to conduct market research to determine if there is a demand for your product or service. In this case, research the demand for coffee vending machines in your area and find out what types of businesses would be the most likely to benefit from having a coffee vending machine on site.

2. Choose a Location

Once you've determined there is a demand for coffee vending machines in your area, it's time to choose a location for your business. Look for high-traffic areas, such as shopping malls, offices, and schools, as these are likely to provide the most opportunities for sales.

3. Purchase Equipment

Next, you'll need to purchase the equipment you need to start your business. This will typically include a coffee vending machine, a supply of coffee beans, cups, and other supplies, as well as any necessary signage.

4. Establish a Supply Chain

In order to ensure you have a steady supply of coffee beans, cups, and other supplies, you'll need to establish a supply chain. This may involve finding a supplier of coffee beans and supplies, as well as securing a regular delivery schedule to ensure you always have what you need on hand.

5. Set Prices

Next, you'll need to set prices for your products. Consider the cost of the equipment, supplies, and delivery, as well as the competition in the area, in order to determine the right price for your products.

6. Market Your Business

Once you have everything in place, it's time to market your business. Consider advertising in local newspapers, on social media, and through local business networks to get the word out about your business. You can also offer discounts and promotions to encourage people to try your products.

7. Monitor Performance

Finally, it's important to monitor the performance of your business in order to make any necessary changes. Regularly review your sales and customer feedback to identify any areas for improvement.

In conclusion, starting a coffee vending machine business can be a rewarding and profitable venture. By conducting market research, choosing the right location, purchasing equipment, establishing a supply chain, setting prices, marketing your business, and monitoring performance, you'll be well on your way to success. With dedication and hard work, you'll be able to grow your business and enjoy the rewards that come with operating your own successful business.

Marketing Your Coffee Vending Machine Business

Marketing is a crucial aspect of any successful business, and your coffee vending machine business is no exception. In this chapter, we'll explore some of the best ways to market your business and grow your customer base.

1. Develop a Strong Brand Identity

A strong brand identity is essential in any business, and this is particularly true in the competitive world of coffee vending machines. Consider developing a memorable logo and tagline, as well as a consistent look and feel for all of your marketing materials.

2. Utilize Social Media

Social media is an excellent way to reach a large audience and promote your business. Consider creating a social media presence for your business and regularly posting updates about new products, promotions, and other news.

3. Offer Promotions and Discounts

Offering promotions and discounts is a great way to encourage people to try your products. Consider offering discounts to new customers, as well as regular promotions to keep your existing customers coming back for more.

4. Collaborate with Other Businesses

Collaborating with other businesses can be an effective way to reach a wider audience and promote your business. Consider partnering with local businesses to offer discounts or special promotions to their customers.

5. Attend Trade Shows and Events

Attending trade shows and events can be a great way to reach a large audience and showcase your products. Consider participating in local events, such as food and beverage fairs, and setting up a booth to promote your business.

6. Utilize Traditional Advertising

In addition to digital marketing, traditional advertising can also be an effective way to reach your target audience. Consider advertising in local newspapers and magazines, as well as on local billboards and other forms of outdoor advertising.

7. Leverage Referral Marketing

Finally, referral marketing can be a powerful tool for growing your customer base. Encourage your satisfied customers to recommend your products to their friends and family, and consider offering incentives for referrals.

In conclusion, marketing your coffee vending machine business is a key factor in its success. By developing a strong brand identity, utilizing social media, offering promotions and discounts, collaborating with other businesses, attending trade shows and events, utilizing traditional advertising, and leveraging referral marketing, you'll be well on your way to reaching a wider audience and growing your customer base.

Creating an Operational Plan for Your Coffee Vending Machine Business

An operational plan is a key component of any successful business, and your coffee vending machine business is no exception. In this chapter, we'll explore the steps you need to take to create an effective operational plan.

1. Define Your Objectives

The first step in creating an operational plan is to define your objectives. This should include both short-term and long-term goals, and should be aligned with your overall business strategy.

2. Assess Your Resources

Once you have defined your objectives, you'll need to assess your resources, including financial, human, and technological resources. This will help you to identify any gaps and make decisions about how to allocate your resources most effectively.

3. Develop Procedures

After you have assessed your resources, you'll need to develop procedures for all aspects of your business, from setting up and maintaining your vending machines, to ordering supplies and handling customer complaints.

4. Allocate Responsibilities

Next, you'll need to allocate responsibilities for each aspect of your business. This includes identifying who will be responsible for each task, as well as establishing clear lines of communication and accountability.

5. Implement Processes for Quality Control

Quality control is a critical aspect of any successful business, and your coffee vending machine business is no exception. Consider implementing processes for quality control, such as regular inspections and maintenance checks, to ensure that your vending machines are always operating at peak performance.

6. Establish Reporting and Monitoring Mechanisms

Finally, you'll need to establish reporting and monitoring mechanisms to ensure that your operational plan is being implemented effectively. This should include regular reporting on key performance indicators, as well as regular assessments of your operational procedures to identify areas for improvement.

In conclusion, creating an operational plan is a key factor in the success of your coffee vending machine business. By defining your objectives, assessing your resources, developing procedures, allocating responsibilities, implementing processes for quality control, and establishing reporting and monitoring mechanisms, you'll be well on your way to a successful and sustainable business.

Developing a business strategy

Developing a Business Strategy for Your Coffee Vending Machine Business

A solid business strategy is essential for the success of your coffee vending machine business. In this chapter, we'll explore the key elements of a successful business strategy and provide tips on how to develop one for your business.

1. Conduct a SWOT Analysis

The first step in developing a business strategy is to conduct a SWOT analysis. SWOT stands for strengths, weaknesses, opportunities, and threats. By identifying these key elements of your business, you'll be able to make informed decisions about your future direction.

2. Identify Your Unique Selling Proposition

Next, you'll need to identify your unique selling proposition (USP). Your USP is what sets your business apart from your competition, and is a key factor in attracting customers. Consider what makes your coffee vending machines unique, and how you can leverage this to your advantage.

3. Define Your Target Market

Defining your target market is a critical part of your business strategy. Consider factors such as location, demographics, and customer needs when determining your target market. Once you have defined your target market, you can tailor your marketing efforts to reach and engage your customers more effectively.

4. Set Realistic Goals

Setting realistic goals is an important part of your business strategy. Consider your short-term and long-term objectives, and establish concrete, measurable goals that align with your overall business strategy.

5. Develop a Marketing Plan

Developing a marketing plan is an essential part of your business strategy. Your marketing plan should include an overview of your target market, your USP, your marketing budget, and a detailed plan for reaching and engaging your target customers.

6. Evaluate and Adjust Your Business Strategy

Finally, it's important to regularly evaluate and adjust your business strategy. Keep track of your key performance indicators, and be open to making changes as needed to ensure that your business strategy remains aligned with your overall goals and objectives.

In conclusion, developing a business strategy is a key factor in the success of your coffee vending machine business. By conducting a SWOT analysis, identifying your USP, defining your target market, setting realistic goals, developing a marketing plan, and regularly evaluating and adjusting your strategy, you'll be well on your way to a successful and sustainable business.

Understanding customer needs

Understanding Customer Needs for Your Coffee Vending Machine Business

One of the most important elements of a successful coffee vending machine business is understanding your customers' needs. In this chapter, we'll explore the key factors you should consider when understanding your customers' needs, and provide tips on how to gather and use customer feedback to inform your business strategy.

1. Location Matters

The location of your coffee vending machines can play a significant role in determining customer needs. For example, a coffee vending machine in a busy office building will likely have different customer needs than one in a university campus. Be sure to consider the unique needs of your target customers when setting up your vending machines.

2. Customer Demographics

Customer demographics, such as age, income, and education level, can also impact customer needs. For example, customers who are in a hurry might appreciate a machine with quick, convenient payment options, while customers who are more health-conscious may prefer a machine that offers a variety of healthy drink options.

3. Customer Feedback

Collecting and using customer feedback is a critical part of understanding your customers' needs. Consider using surveys, customer satisfaction ratings, and direct feedback from customers to gather valuable insights into their needs and preferences.

4. Market Trends

Keeping up-to-date with market trends is also important when understanding your customers' needs. Consider conducting market research to identify any shifts in customer preferences or trends in the coffee vending machine industry.

5. Product Offerings

Your product offerings can also impact customer needs. Consider offering a variety of drinks, including coffee, tea, hot chocolate, and cold drinks, to meet the needs of different customers. Additionally, consider offering different sizes, flavors, and sweeteners to accommodate different tastes and preferences.

6. Payment Options

Finally, payment options can play a significant role in determining customer needs. Offer a variety of payment options, such as cash, credit cards, and mobile payments, to make the vending machine experience as convenient and accessible as possible for your customers.

In conclusion, understanding customer needs is essential for the success of your coffee vending machine business. By considering location, customer demographics, feedback, market trends, product offerings, and payment options, you'll be able to offer a product and service that meets the needs and preferences of your target customers.

Calculating costs and revenue

Calculating Costs and Revenue for Your Coffee Vending Machine Business

As with any business, it's essential to understand your costs and revenue to determine the financial viability of your coffee vending machine business. In this chapter, we'll provide an overview of the key costs and revenue factors to consider when calculating your business finances.

1. Initial Investment Costs

The initial investment costs for a coffee vending machine business can include the cost of purchasing or leasing vending machines, installation costs, and any other setup costs such as signage and marketing materials. Be sure to carefully consider these costs when determining your initial investment budget.

2. Ongoing Operating Costs

Ongoing operating costs for a coffee vending machine business can include electricity and maintenance costs, as well as the cost of supplies such as coffee, cups, and other vending machine essentials. Be sure to factor these costs into your budget when calculating your expected revenue.

3. Product Pricing

Product pricing is a key factor in determining your revenue potential. Consider the costs of your supplies and operating expenses when determining the prices you will charge for your drinks. Be mindful of market trends and competition when setting your prices to ensure you remain competitive and profitable.

4. Volume Sales

Volume sales can impact both your costs and revenue. The more vending machines you have in operation, the more drinks you will sell and the higher your revenue potential will be. However, it's essential to balance the number of machines with the cost of maintaining and operating them to ensure profitability.

5. Payment Processing Fees

Payment processing fees, such as credit card fees, can also impact your revenue. Be sure to factor these fees into your pricing strategy and budget to ensure you are able to remain profitable while offering convenient payment options to your customers.

6. Marketing and Advertising Costs

Marketing and advertising costs can also impact your costs and revenue. Consider developing a marketing strategy that targets your target customers and helps to drive traffic to your vending machines. Be mindful of your budget and focus on cost-effective marketing techniques to maximize your return on investment.

In conclusion, understanding your costs and revenue is essential for the success of your coffee vending machine business. By considering your initial investment costs, ongoing operating costs, product pricing, volume sales, payment processing fees, and marketing and advertising costs, you'll be able to develop a budget and business plan that will help you achieve your financial goals.

Keeping track of sales

Keeping Track of Sales for Your Coffee Vending Machine Business

Keeping accurate records of your sales is essential for the success of your coffee vending machine business. In this chapter, we'll provide an overview of the key factors to consider when tracking your sales and managing your finances.

1. Sales Tracking Software

One of the most effective ways to keep track of your sales is to use sales tracking software. Many coffee vending machine manufacturers offer sales tracking software that integrates with their vending machines, allowing you to monitor sales and inventory in real-time.

2. Sales Reports

Regular sales reports can help you keep track of your overall sales performance. These reports can provide valuable insights into which drinks are selling the most, as well as which vending machines are performing the best.

3. Inventory Management

Inventory management is a critical aspect of sales tracking. Regularly monitoring your inventory levels will help you ensure that you always have enough supplies on hand to meet customer demand.

4. Payment Processing Records

Keeping accurate records of your payment processing transactions is also essential. This information can help you reconcile your sales reports and ensure that all payments have been properly processed.

5. Financial Statements

Regular financial statements, such as balance sheets and income statements, can help you track your business's financial performance over time. These statements can provide valuable insights into your overall revenue, expenses, and profits, allowing you to make informed decisions about your business's future.

In conclusion, keeping accurate records of your sales and finances is critical for the success of your coffee vending machine business. By using sales tracking software, generating sales reports, monitoring your inventory levels, keeping accurate payment processing records, and regularly reviewing your financial statements, you'll be able to stay on top of your finances and make informed decisions about your business's future.

Building customer loyalty

Building Customer Loyalty for Your Coffee Vending Machine Business

Building customer loyalty is essential for the long-term success of your coffee vending machine business. In this chapter, we'll explore some strategies you can use to build customer loyalty and keep your customers coming back.

1. Provide High-Quality Products and Services

The first step in building customer loyalty is to provide high-quality products and services. Customers are more likely to return to a business that consistently provides them with good quality coffee, fast and convenient service, and a pleasant overall experience.

2. Offer Customization Options

Offering customization options, such as the ability to select different coffee strengths and flavors, can help you meet the unique needs of your customers. This can help differentiate your business from the competition and increase customer loyalty.

3. Provide Exceptional Customer Service

Providing exceptional customer service is also key to building customer loyalty. This can include responding promptly to customer inquiries and complaints, offering friendly and helpful service, and going above and beyond to make customers happy.

4. Implement a Rewards Program

Implementing a rewards program can help you incentivize customers to continue using your vending machines. This can include offering discounts, free drinks, or other incentives for repeat customers.

5. Foster a Sense of Community

Fostering a sense of community can also help you build customer loyalty. This can include hosting events or offering special promotions to customers who regularly use your vending machines.

In conclusion, building customer loyalty is essential for the long-term success of your coffee vending machine business. By providing high-quality products and services, offering customization options, providing exceptional customer service, implementing a rewards program, and fostering a sense of community, you'll be able to build customer loyalty and keep your customers coming back.

Staying ahead of the competition

Staying Ahead of the Competition in the Coffee Vending
Machine Business

In any market, competition is always a factor that business
owners need to take into account. In the coffee vending
machine business, competition can be especially fierce, with
many different players vying for customers. In this chapter,
we'll explore some strategies you can use to stay ahead of the
competition and maintain your competitive edge.

1. Stay Up-to-Date with Industry Trends

Staying up-to-date with industry trends is key to staying
ahead of the competition. This can include attending trade
shows and conferences, reading industry publications, and
researching your competition to see what they're doing. By
staying up-to-date, you can identify new opportunities and
stay ahead of your competition.

2. Offer Unique Products and Services

Offering unique products and services is another way to stay
ahead of the competition. This can include offering special
flavors of coffee or innovative vending machine features that
set your business apart from the competition.

3. Provide Superior Customer Service

Providing superior customer service is also key to staying
ahead of the competition. This can include responding
promptly to customer inquiries and complaints, offering

friendly and helpful service, and going above and beyond to make customers happy.

4. Focus on Marketing and Advertising

Focusing on marketing and advertising can also help you stay ahead of the competition. This can include creating eye-catching vending machine displays, using social media to reach customers, and developing targeted advertising campaigns to reach your target audience.

5. Invest in Technology

Investing in technology is another way to stay ahead of the competition. This can include implementing new software and hardware solutions that help you streamline your business and improve customer experience.

In conclusion, staying ahead of the competition is essential for the long-term success of your coffee vending machine business. By staying up-to-date with industry trends, offering unique products and services, providing superior customer service, focusing on marketing and advertising, and investing in technology, you'll be able to maintain your competitive edge and stay ahead of the competition.

Meeting industry standards and regulations

Meeting Industry Standards and Regulations for Coffee Vending Machines

In the coffee vending machine industry, it's important to be aware of the various standards and regulations that must be met in order to operate a successful business. Failure to meet these standards and regulations can result in fines, legal action, and damage to your reputation. In this chapter, we'll explore some of the key standards and regulations that coffee vending machine businesses must abide by.

1. Health and Safety Standards

Health and safety standards are one of the most important considerations in the coffee vending machine industry. This includes ensuring that vending machines are clean and hygienic, that they are equipped with proper ventilation, and that they are free from hazards such as sharp edges or exposed electrical wires.

2. Quality Standards

Quality standards are also important in the coffee vending machine industry. This includes ensuring that vending machines are well-maintained, that they produce high-quality coffee, and that they are equipped with reliable and efficient equipment.

3. Energy Efficiency Standards

Energy efficiency standards are another important consideration in the coffee vending machine industry. This includes ensuring that vending machines are designed to be energy-efficient and that they use environmentally-friendly materials and processes.

4. Payment System Standards

Payment system standards are also important in the coffee vending machine industry. This includes ensuring that vending machines are equipped with secure and reliable payment systems, such as card readers or mobile payment options.

5. Legal Requirements

Legal requirements are also an important consideration in the coffee vending machine industry. This includes ensuring that vending machines are properly licensed and registered, that they comply with all relevant laws and regulations, and that they are insured against liability.

In conclusion, meeting industry standards and regulations is essential for the success of your coffee vending machine business. By adhering to health and safety standards, quality standards, energy efficiency standards, payment system standards, and legal requirements, you'll be able to operate a safe, efficient, and successful business that meets all of the necessary requirements.

Managing employees and finances

Managing Employees and Finances in Your Coffee Vending
Machine Business

Running a successful coffee vending machine business
requires careful management of both employees and finances.
In this chapter, we'll explore some of the key considerations
for managing employees and finances in the coffee vending
machine industry.

1. Employee Management

Employee management is an important aspect of running a
coffee vending machine business. This includes recruiting and
training employees, setting schedules, monitoring
performance, and ensuring that employees are paid fairly and
on time. In addition, it's important to have clear policies in
place for handling issues such as absenteeism, lateness, and
misconduct.

2. Financial Management

Financial management is also a critical aspect of running a
coffee vending machine business. This includes tracking
income and expenses, preparing budgets, and keeping
accurate financial records. In addition, it's important to have a
clear understanding of the various tax laws and regulations
that apply to your business.

3. Budgeting

Budgeting is a key component of financial management in the coffee vending machine industry. This involves setting aside funds for various expenses such as rent, utilities, supplies, and equipment maintenance. It's also important to set aside funds for marketing and advertising, as well as for any unexpected expenses that may arise.

4. Record Keeping

Record keeping is another important aspect of financial management in the coffee vending machine industry. This includes keeping accurate records of all income and expenses, as well as maintaining accurate records of all transactions. This information is critical for preparing financial statements, tracking progress, and making informed business decisions.

5. Cash Management

Cash management is also an important aspect of running a coffee vending machine business. This includes ensuring that vending machines have adequate cash supplies, that cash is handled securely, and that cash is deposited into the bank in a timely manner.

In conclusion, managing employees and finances is essential for the success of your coffee vending machine business. By effectively managing employees, finances, budgets, record keeping, and cash management, you'll be able to operate a profitable and efficient business that is well-positioned for long-term success.

Offering different coffee blends and flavors

Offering Different Coffee Blends and Flavors in Your Coffee Vending Machine Business

One of the keys to success in the coffee vending machine business is offering a variety of coffee blends and flavors that meet the needs and preferences of your customers. In this chapter, we'll explore some of the key considerations for offering different coffee blends and flavors in the coffee vending machine industry.

1. Understanding Your Customers

The first step in offering different coffee blends and flavors is to understand your customers. This includes learning about their coffee preferences, such as the type of coffee they like (e.g. dark roast, light roast, medium roast), their preferred flavor profiles (e.g. chocolate, caramel, vanilla), and the type of milk or creamer they prefer. By understanding your customers, you'll be better equipped to offer coffee blends and flavors that meet their needs and preferences.

2. Offering a Variety of Coffee Blends

Offering a variety of coffee blends is an important aspect of the coffee vending machine business. This includes offering a range of roasts (e.g. dark, light, medium), as well as a range of flavor profiles (e.g. chocolate, caramel, vanilla). By offering a variety of coffee blends, you'll be able to attract a broader range of customers, and increase the chances of customers returning to your vending machine.

3. Offering Specialty Drinks

In addition to offering a variety of coffee blends, it's also important to offer specialty drinks. This includes popular drinks such as lattes, cappuccinos, and macchiatos. By offering specialty drinks, you'll be able to attract customers who are looking for a more specialized coffee experience.

4. Working with Coffee Suppliers

When offering different coffee blends and flavors, it's important to work with reliable coffee suppliers. This includes selecting suppliers who offer high-quality coffee beans, and who are able to provide consistent supplies of coffee beans. By working with reliable coffee suppliers, you'll be able to ensure that your vending machines are always stocked with the coffee blends and flavors that your customers prefer.

In conclusion, offering different coffee blends and flavors is essential for the success of your coffee vending machine business. By understanding your customers, offering a variety of coffee blends, offering specialty drinks, and working with reliable coffee suppliers, you'll be able to offer a range of coffee blends and flavors that meet the needs and preferences of your customers, and increase the chances of customers returning to your vending machine.

Maintaining the quality of coffee and supplies

Maintaining the quality of your coffee and supplies is critical to the success of your coffee vending machine business. Here are some tips to help you keep the quality of your coffee and supplies at its best.

1. Choose the Right Coffee Beans: The quality of your coffee will depend largely on the type of coffee beans you use. It's essential to choose high-quality coffee beans from a reputable supplier. Do your research, taste test different blends, and choose the one that best meets the needs and preferences of your customers.
2. Store Coffee Beans Properly: Once you have chosen the right coffee beans, store them in an airtight container in a cool, dry place. This will help preserve the freshness and flavor of your coffee.
3. Regular Cleaning: Regular cleaning of your coffee vending machine is important to ensure the quality of your coffee. Cleaning should be done regularly to remove any buildup of coffee oils, which can affect the taste of your coffee.
4. Keep Supplies Fresh: Keep your supplies, such as sugar, creamer, and cups, fresh by regularly checking expiration dates and replacing any expired items. This will help ensure the quality of your coffee and keep your customers happy.
5. Regular Maintenance: Regular maintenance of your coffee vending machine is crucial to ensure it continues to perform optimally. Regularly check for any wear and tear and make repairs as necessary.

By following these tips, you can maintain the quality of your coffee and supplies and keep your customers coming back for more. Remember, the quality of your coffee and supplies will play a crucial role in the success of your coffee vending machine business, so make sure to prioritize it.

Developing Partnerships with Suppliers

Developing partnerships with suppliers is an important aspect of running a successful coffee vending machine business. By working closely with suppliers, you can ensure a steady supply of high-quality coffee beans, supplies, and equipment, while also gaining access to valuable insights and support. Here are some tips to help you develop strong partnerships with suppliers.

1. Choose the Right Suppliers: When selecting suppliers, look for those with a strong reputation for quality and reliability. Research different suppliers and take the time to get to know them, their products, and their services.
2. Build Relationships: Building strong relationships with your suppliers is key to a successful partnership. Regular communication, transparency, and mutual respect are important components of a healthy supplier relationship.
3. Negotiate Contracts: When working with suppliers, it's important to have a clear and mutually agreed-upon contract in place. This can help ensure the terms of the partnership are clear and that both parties are committed to meeting their obligations.
4. Stay Current with Industry Trends: Stay up-to-date with industry trends and changes in the coffee vending machine market. This will help you make informed decisions and better understand the needs of your customers, which in turn will help you negotiate better deals with suppliers.
5. Collaborate on Marketing and Promotions: Working with suppliers on marketing and promotions can help boost your business and increase sales. Consider

collaborating on joint promotions or special deals, which can help draw in new customers and increase brand awareness.

By following these tips, you can develop strong partnerships with suppliers that will help you grow and succeed in the coffee vending machine business. Remember, building and maintaining good relationships with suppliers is key to a successful business, so make sure to prioritize this aspect of your operations.

Managing Cash Flow and Expenses

As a coffee vending machine business owner, it's essential to effectively manage your cash flow and expenses to ensure long-term success. Here are some tips to help you do just that:

1. Create a budget: Developing a budget will give you a clear picture of your expected income and expenses. This will help you plan for future expenditures and ensure that you have enough cash to cover your expenses.
2. Track expenses: Keep accurate records of all your expenses, including those for supplies, maintenance, and any other costs associated with running your business.
3. Evaluate expenses regularly: Review your expenses regularly to identify areas where you can cut costs or reduce spending. This could include negotiating better deals with suppliers or finding more cost-effective solutions for maintenance and upkeep.
4. Manage inventory: Make sure to manage your inventory effectively to avoid overstocking or running out of supplies. This will help you keep costs under control and ensure that your customers always have access to the products they want.
5. Utilize technology: Take advantage of technology to streamline your financial management processes. Consider using accounting software to automate your bookkeeping and make it easier to track your expenses and cash flow.
6. Seek advice: If you're having trouble managing your finances, don't be afraid to seek advice from a financial expert or accountant. They can provide you with

valuable insights and help you find solutions to any financial challenges you may be facing.

By following these tips and paying close attention to your cash flow and expenses, you'll be well on your way to a successful and sustainable coffee vending machine business.

Investing in Research and Development

Investing in research and development (R&D) is crucial for the success and growth of your coffee vending machine business. This involves constantly seeking out new technologies, products, and services to enhance your offerings and stay ahead of the competition.

Here are a few benefits of investing in R&D:

1. Improved customer satisfaction: By investing in R&D, you can ensure that your coffee vending machines offer the latest technology and best possible experience for your customers. From improved brewing methods to enhanced interfaces, you can keep your customers coming back for more.
2. Competitive advantage: By staying ahead of the curve with the latest advancements in coffee vending technology, you can differentiate yourself from your competitors and increase your chances of success.
3. Increased revenue: With a constant stream of new and innovative products, you can increase your revenue by attracting new customers and retaining existing ones.

When investing in R&D, it's important to consider the following:

1. Budget: Set aside a budget for R&D that allows for a balance between immediate results and long-term growth.
2. Timing: Decide when to invest in R&D based on the needs of your business. If you're just starting out, it may

be more beneficial to focus on establishing a solid foundation first.
3. Collaboration: Partner with coffee suppliers and vending machine manufacturers to develop new and innovative products that meet the needs of your customers.

By investing in R&D, you can stay ahead of the competition and ensure the long-term success of your coffee vending machine business. So, don't be afraid to think outside the box and invest in the future of your business!

Keeping up with Industry Trends

As a coffee vending machine business owner, it's important to stay informed of the latest developments in the industry and be proactive in incorporating them into your business. Doing so will help you stay ahead of the competition and continue to grow your business. Here are some tips on how to keep up with industry trends:

1. Attend industry conferences and trade shows: Attending industry events is a great way to learn about new products, innovations, and emerging trends. You'll have the opportunity to network with other professionals and suppliers and gain valuable insights into the industry.
2. Read industry publications: Keeping up with industry publications, such as trade magazines, is a great way to stay informed of the latest developments and trends in the coffee vending machine industry.
3. Follow industry leaders: Following industry leaders and influencers on social media, blogs, and other platforms can provide valuable insights into emerging trends and best practices.
4. Monitor customer feedback: Listening to your customers' feedback can give you an idea of the latest trends and demands in the market. This information can help you tailor your offerings and make informed decisions about new products and services.
5. Conduct market research: Conducting regular market research can provide valuable insights into customer needs, market trends, and industry developments. You

can use this information to inform your business strategy and make informed decisions.

Staying ahead of the competition and keeping up with industry trends is essential for the success of your coffee vending machine business. By incorporating new innovations and trends into your business, you'll be able to provide your customers with the best products and services and stay ahead of the curve.

Expanding your business to new locations

Expanding your coffee vending machine business to new locations is a great way to increase your revenue and reach new customers. However, it's important to approach expansion carefully and methodically. In this chapter, we'll cover some tips and best practices for expanding your coffee vending machine business to new locations.

1. Conduct Market Research: Before expanding to a new location, it's important to research the local market to understand consumer demand and competition. Identify potential locations that have a high traffic flow and a strong customer base. Consider factors such as demographics, purchasing patterns, and consumer preferences in your research.
2. Evaluate Costs: Expanding your business to a new location requires a significant investment, including costs for equipment, supplies, marketing, and staffing. Make sure you have a solid financial plan in place and that you have the necessary funding to support the expansion.
3. Partner with Local Businesses: Partnering with local businesses can be a great way to establish a presence in a new location. Consider partnering with coffee shops, cafes, or other food and beverage establishments to offer your coffee vending machine services to their customers.
4. Hire the Right Team: Hiring the right team is key to successfully expanding your business to a new location. Look for experienced and knowledgeable employees who are passionate about coffee and customer service. Provide comprehensive training for your new

employees to ensure that they are equipped to provide the best possible customer experience.

5. Establish a Strong Marketing Strategy: Establishing a strong marketing strategy is crucial to getting the word out about your coffee vending machine business in a new location. Consider using social media, advertising, and local events to reach potential customers. Offer special promotions or discounts to attract customers and build brand awareness.

6. Monitor Progress: Once you've established a presence in a new location, it's important to monitor progress and make adjustments as needed. Regularly track sales and customer feedback to make sure that you are meeting customer needs and expectations.

Expanding your coffee vending machine business to new locations can be a great way to increase your revenue and reach new customers. By conducting market research, evaluating costs, partnering with local businesses, hiring the right team, and establishing a strong marketing strategy, you can set your business up for success. Remember to monitor progress and make adjustments as needed to ensure that your business continues to grow and thrive in new locations.

Building Brand Awareness

Introduction: In today's highly competitive market, it's essential for businesses to stand out and establish a strong brand image. Building brand awareness is crucial for the success of a coffee vending machine business as it helps to attract new customers, retain existing ones, and increase profitability. A well-established brand can also enhance your company's reputation and provide a competitive advantage.

1. Define your brand identity: Start by defining your brand identity, including your brand values, mission, and vision. This will help you create a clear and consistent brand image and messaging, which is essential for building brand awareness.
2. Utilize social media: Social media platforms are a powerful tool for building brand awareness and reaching a large audience. Make use of platforms such as Facebook, Instagram, and Twitter to share updates, promotions, and relevant content.
3. Offer exceptional customer service: Providing excellent customer service is a great way to build brand awareness and establish a positive reputation. Encourage customers to leave positive reviews on your social media pages and respond promptly to any negative feedback.
4. Participate in local events: Participating in local events such as fairs, festivals, and trade shows is a great way to increase brand visibility and interact with potential customers. This will also help you to network with other businesses and establish relationships with key stakeholders in the community.

5. Develop partnerships: Partnering with other businesses in your industry can help you increase brand exposure and reach new customers. Consider partnering with local cafes, restaurants, or hotels to offer your coffee vending machine services.

6. Offer promotions and discounts: Offering promotions and discounts is a great way to attract new customers and increase brand awareness. You can offer special deals for first-time customers, loyalty programs, or seasonal promotions to keep your brand fresh in the minds of your customers.

Conclusion: Building brand awareness is a crucial aspect of growing a successful coffee vending machine business. By consistently providing exceptional customer service, utilizing social media, participating in local events, developing partnerships, and offering promotions and discounts, you can establish a strong brand image and increase visibility in the market. Keep in mind that building brand awareness takes time and effort, but with persistence and hard work, you can establish a thriving and profitable business.

Offering promotions and discounts

In the competitive world of coffee vending machine businesses, it is important to differentiate yourself from your competitors. One way to do this is by offering promotions and discounts to your customers. Promotions and discounts can help attract new customers, retain existing customers, and increase sales.

There are several types of promotions and discounts that you can offer, including:

1. Seasonal promotions: Offer promotions during holidays or special events, such as Christmas, Valentine's Day, or National Coffee Day.
2. Loyalty programs: Reward your regular customers with discounts or special promotions for their loyalty.
3. BOGO (buy one, get one) deals: Offer customers a discount or a free item when they purchase a coffee vending machine drink.
4. Referral discounts: Offer customers a discount or a free item when they refer a friend or family member to your business.
5. Limited-time promotions: Offer promotions for a limited time to create a sense of urgency and encourage customers to make a purchase.

When developing promotions and discounts, it is important to consider your target audience and the types of promotions and discounts they are likely to respond to. For example, younger customers may be more likely to respond to promotions through social media, while older customers may prefer traditional advertising methods, such as flyers or billboards.

It is also important to consider your budget when offering promotions and discounts. While promotions and discounts can increase sales, they can also reduce your profits. Therefore, it is important to find a balance between offering promotions and discounts and maintaining a profitable business.

In conclusion, promotions and discounts can be a valuable tool for attracting and retaining customers, increasing sales, and differentiating your business from your competitors. When developing and offering promotions and discounts, it is important to consider your target audience, budget, and overall business goals.

Implementing customer feedback

As a coffee vending machine business owner, one of the most important things you can do is listen to your customers. By understanding their needs, wants, and concerns, you can make improvements to your business that will keep them coming back for more. Here's how to get started with implementing customer feedback.

1. Ask for feedback: The first step in implementing customer feedback is to ask for it. You can do this by sending out surveys, hosting focus groups, or simply asking customers directly. Whatever method you choose, make sure that you make it easy for customers to share their thoughts.
2. Analyze the data: Once you've received feedback, it's time to analyze the data. Look for common themes and patterns in the responses. This will help you identify areas where you can make improvements.
3. Develop a plan: Based on the feedback you've received, develop a plan to make changes to your business. Make a list of the changes you want to make and prioritize them based on their importance.
4. Take action: The next step is to take action. Start implementing the changes you've identified. If you're making a big change, like adding a new coffee blend or updating your vending machine, make sure to communicate the change to your customers.
5. Evaluate your progress: After you've made the changes, evaluate your progress. Ask your customers for feedback again and see if they're satisfied with the

changes you've made. If not, keep making changes until you get it right.

Implementing customer feedback is a continuous process. It's important to regularly ask for feedback and make changes based on what your customers are saying. By doing this, you'll build a loyal customer base and keep your business growing.

Evaluating Business Performance

As a coffee vending machine business owner, it's important to regularly assess your business performance to see what's working well and what needs improvement. This will help you make informed decisions that will drive your business forward. Here are some key areas to focus on when evaluating your business performance:

1. Sales and revenue: Look at your sales figures over a set period of time (monthly, quarterly, annually, etc.) to see how much revenue you're generating. This will give you a good indication of the overall health of your business and help you determine whether you need to make any changes to your business strategy.

2. Customer satisfaction: It's important to regularly survey your customers to get their feedback on your coffee vending machines and the overall customer experience. Use this information to make improvements and build customer loyalty.

3. Employee satisfaction: Regularly check in with your employees to see how they're feeling about their work and their relationship with the company. A happy workforce is essential to the success of your business.

4. Operational efficiency: Evaluate how efficiently your coffee vending machines are operating. Are they frequently out of order or in need of repairs? This could be an indication that it's time to invest in new equipment or better maintenance processes.

5. Competitor analysis: Keep an eye on your competitors to see what they're doing differently and what you can

learn from their strategies. This will help you stay ahead of the competition and stay relevant in the market.

By regularly evaluating your business performance, you'll be able to make informed decisions that will help your coffee vending machine business grow and succeed. Don't be afraid to make changes where necessary and always strive to improve. With dedication and hard work, you'll see your business reach new heights!

Improving Customer Service

Introduction:

Customer service is a critical aspect of any business, including a coffee vending machine business. Happy customers lead to repeat business and positive word of mouth, while poor customer service can quickly damage a company's reputation. In this chapter, we will look at ways to improve customer service and enhance the overall experience for customers.

Listening to customer feedback:

One of the best ways to improve customer service is to listen to customer feedback. This feedback can come from various sources, including customer reviews, surveys, and personal interactions. It's important to take customer feedback seriously, respond to it promptly, and use it to make meaningful improvements to the business.

Providing prompt and efficient service:

Customers expect a quick and seamless experience when using a coffee vending machine. Ensure that the vending machines are well-maintained and fully stocked, and that any issues are resolved as quickly as possible. Offer a clear and concise menu, and make sure the process of purchasing a coffee is straightforward and easy to follow.

Training employees:

Employees are the face of the business, and it's important that they are trained in providing excellent customer service. Teach employees how to handle customer complaints and resolve issues quickly and efficiently. Ensure that employees are knowledgeable about the products and services offered, and encourage them to be friendly and approachable.

Offering value-added services:

Consider offering additional services or products that will enhance the customer experience, such as free Wi-Fi or complementary snacks. These value-added services will help differentiate your business from competitors and make customers more likely to choose your vending machines over others.

Conclusion:

Improving customer service is an ongoing process that requires attention and effort. By listening to customer feedback, providing efficient service, training employees, offering value-added services, and continuously evaluating performance, a coffee vending machine business can provide a positive customer experience and build a loyal customer base.

Establishing a Training Program for Employees

When it comes to running a successful coffee vending machine business, having a team of well-trained employees is crucial. Not only does it ensure that your customers receive the best possible experience, but it also helps streamline operations, minimize errors, and improve overall efficiency.

To achieve this, it's important to establish a comprehensive training program for your employees. This program should cover all aspects of the job, from the basics of operating the vending machine to more advanced skills such as customer service, inventory management, and troubleshooting.

Here are some key steps for establishing an effective training program:

1. Define the objective: Start by defining what you want to achieve with the training program. This could be anything from improving customer service to increasing sales. Having a clear objective in mind will help you create a more focused and effective program.
2. Identify the training needs: Based on your objective, identify the specific skills and knowledge that your employees will need to be successful in their role. This could include machine operation, customer service, inventory management, and more.
3. Develop the content: Based on the training needs, create a comprehensive training manual that covers all the relevant topics. This manual should include step-by-step instructions, images, videos, and other materials

that will help your employees understand and apply the information.

4. Choose a delivery method: Consider the best way to deliver the training to your employees. This could be in-person training, online training, or a combination of both. Keep in mind that different employees may have different learning styles, so try to offer a variety of delivery methods to accommodate everyone.
5. Set a timeline: Decide when you want to launch the training program and set a timeline for completion. This will help ensure that your employees are trained in a timely manner and that the program doesn't get pushed to the backburner.
6. Monitor progress: Continuously monitor your employees' progress throughout the training program and make adjustments as needed. This will help you identify areas where employees may be struggling and provide additional support where needed.

By implementing a comprehensive training program for your employees, you'll not only improve their skills and knowledge, but you'll also help ensure the success of your coffee vending machine business. Whether you're just starting out or looking to improve your existing program, these steps can help you establish a training program that works for your team.

Upgrading Coffee Vending Machines

Coffee vending machines play a crucial role in many businesses. As technology evolves, it is important to keep up with the latest advancements in order to stay ahead of the competition and provide the best possible service to customers. In this chapter, we will explore the various ways you can upgrade your coffee vending machines and the benefits of doing so.

Benefits of Upgrading

There are many benefits to upgrading your coffee vending machines. First and foremost, upgrading can help you stay ahead of the competition. The latest coffee vending machines come with improved features and options, such as better brewing systems, larger and more vibrant displays, and increased storage capacity. Upgrading can also help you attract new customers by providing them with a more modern and enjoyable experience.

Another important benefit of upgrading is increased efficiency. Newer coffee vending machines are designed to be more efficient in terms of energy consumption, water usage, and maintenance. This can help reduce costs and increase profitability over the long term. Additionally, many newer coffee vending machines are equipped with sensors and software that can provide real-time data on usage, performance, and maintenance needs, making it easier to manage your business.

Factors to Consider

Before upgrading your coffee vending machines, there are several factors to consider. The first is the cost of the upgrade. Upgrading can be expensive, so it is important to consider your budget and find the best solution for your needs. You should also consider the compatibility of the new machines with your existing systems and infrastructure, as well as the installation process and any required training for employees.

Another important factor to consider is the type of coffee vending machine you are using. There are many different types of coffee vending machines, each with its own strengths and weaknesses. It is important to choose the right type of machine for your needs, taking into account factors such as the volume of coffee you need to dispense, the type of customers you serve, and your budget.

Finally, it is important to consider the features and options you need. Some of the latest coffee vending machines come with features such as adjustable temperature control, customizable menus, and touch screen displays. These features can help improve the customer experience, but they also come at a premium cost.

Choosing the Right Upgrade

When choosing the right upgrade for your coffee vending machines, it is important to consider your needs and budget. You may choose to upgrade your existing machines, or you may choose to purchase new machines entirely. If you are upgrading your existing machines, consider what specific improvements you need, such as a better brewing system, larger storage capacity, or a more user-friendly interface.

If you are purchasing new machines, there are several options to consider. Some of the latest coffee vending machines are equipped with cutting-edge technology such as high-resolution displays, automatic brewing systems, and advanced software for real-time data analysis. Other machines may be designed for specific types of customers, such as those who prefer specialty coffees or those who need a machine that can dispense hot and cold beverages.

Conclusion

Upgrading your coffee vending machines can provide many benefits, including increased efficiency, improved customer experience, and increased profitability. When choosing the right upgrade, it is important to consider your needs, budget, and the type of machine you are using. With the right upgrade, you can stay ahead of the competition and provide the best possible service to your customers.

Building a Company Culture

Introduction: A strong company culture is essential for any business, especially in the coffee vending machine industry. It helps to define the values, beliefs, and behaviors that employees are expected to exhibit. A positive company culture can enhance employee satisfaction, reduce turnover, and improve overall performance.

What is Company Culture? Company culture refers to the personality and character of a business. It is shaped by the company's mission, values, and beliefs, as well as the attitudes and behaviors of its employees. The culture of a business can be expressed through its physical surroundings, communication style, and overall approach to work.

Why is Company Culture Important? A strong company culture can be a competitive advantage. When employees feel connected to the company and its values, they are more likely to be engaged, productive, and committed to the company's success. A positive company culture also helps to attract and retain talent, which is essential for growth and success in the long term.

How to Build a Company Culture:

1. Establish a clear mission and values: Develop a clear mission statement and core values that reflect the company's purpose and goals. These should be communicated to employees and incorporated into all aspects of the business.
2. Foster a positive work environment: Create a work environment that is positive, supportive, and inclusive.

This can include offering flexible schedules, providing opportunities for professional growth and development, and recognizing and rewarding employee contributions.

3. Encourage open communication: Encourage open and honest communication between employees and management. This can include regular check-ins, town hall meetings, and feedback sessions.

4. Promote teamwork: Encourage collaboration and teamwork among employees. This can include team-building activities, cross-functional projects, and opportunities for employees to work together.

5. Lead by example: Company leaders should embody the company's values and mission in their actions and behaviors. They should be approachable and accessible, and actively seek feedback from employees.

6. Continuously evaluate and improve: Regularly evaluate the company culture and make changes as needed. This can include conducting surveys, seeking feedback from employees, and making changes based on that feedback.

Conclusion: Building a strong company culture is essential for success in the coffee vending machine industry. By establishing clear values and goals, fostering a positive work environment, and promoting teamwork and open communication, you can create a culture that supports employee engagement and performance. Regularly evaluating and improving your company culture will ensure that it remains relevant and effective in supporting your business over time.

Developing a Crisis Management Plan

As a business owner, it's important to be prepared for any crisis that may arise. A well-defined crisis management plan can help you respond effectively to unexpected events and minimize the damage to your business. Here are some key steps to help you develop a crisis management plan for your coffee vending machine business.

1. Identify potential crises

The first step in developing a crisis management plan is to identify the types of crises that your business could potentially face. This could include anything from natural disasters to equipment malfunctions, theft, or cyber attacks. Make a list of all the potential crises that your business could face and prioritize them based on their likelihood and potential impact.

2. Assign roles and responsibilities

Once you have identified potential crises, you need to assign specific roles and responsibilities to your employees. This will help ensure that everyone knows what to do in the event of a crisis. For example, you may want to designate a point person who will be responsible for coordinating the response, a communications manager who will handle media inquiries, and a recovery manager who will lead the effort to get the business back up and running.

3. Develop response procedures

Based on the types of crises you've identified, you need to develop specific response procedures. This could include evacuating the building, shutting down certain systems, or communicating with customers. Make sure your procedures are clear, concise, and easy to follow. You should also conduct regular training sessions to ensure that all employees know how to respond in the event of a crisis.

4. Establish a communication plan

Effective communication is key during a crisis. You need to have a plan in place for communicating with employees, customers, suppliers, and other stakeholders. This should include contact information for key personnel, a protocol for communicating important updates, and a plan for using social media and other digital channels to get the word out.

5. Review and update your plan regularly

Finally, it's important to regularly review and update your crisis management plan. This will help ensure that it remains relevant and effective, and that you're prepared for any new types of crises that may arise. You should also conduct regular drills and simulations to test your response procedures and make any necessary adjustments.

In conclusion, a well-defined crisis management plan is a critical component of any successful business. By following the steps outlined above, you can ensure that your coffee vending machine business is prepared to respond effectively to any crisis that may arise.

Managing risks and challenges

Managing Risks and Challenges in a Coffee Vending Machine Business

Starting and running a coffee vending machine business can be exciting, but it also comes with a set of challenges and risks. As an entrepreneur, it is important to anticipate and prepare for potential obstacles that may arise. This chapter will help you understand how to manage risks and overcome challenges in your business.

1. Market competition One of the biggest challenges that you may face is market competition. With the increasing popularity of coffee vending machines, the number of competitors in the market has also increased. To stay ahead of the competition, it is important to offer unique and high-quality coffee blends, exceptional customer service, and competitive pricing.
2. Economic downturns The economy can be volatile, and economic downturns can affect the demand for coffee vending machines. To prepare for this, it is important to have a robust financial plan and a diverse customer base. This will help ensure that your business remains profitable, even during tough economic times.
3. Changes in customer preferences Customers' preferences and tastes can change over time, so it is important to stay up-to-date with industry trends and continuously offer new and innovative coffee blends. Keeping an open line of communication with your customers can also help you understand their evolving needs and preferences.

4. Machine breakdowns and maintenance Coffee vending machines require regular maintenance to ensure they are in good working condition. Machine breakdowns can lead to customer dissatisfaction and lost revenue. To minimize the impact of machine breakdowns, it is important to invest in high-quality machines and have a regular maintenance schedule in place.

5. Employee turnover Employee turnover can be a challenge for any business, and it can be especially challenging in the coffee vending machine industry. To mitigate this risk, it is important to have a robust employee training program, offer competitive compensation and benefits packages, and foster a positive work environment.

6. Regulatory compliance The coffee vending machine industry is regulated by government agencies, and it is important to understand and comply with all relevant regulations. Failure to comply with regulations can result in fines, legal action, and damage to your reputation.

In conclusion, managing risks and challenges in a coffee vending machine business requires careful planning and preparation. By anticipating potential obstacles, you can develop strategies to minimize their impact and ensure the success of your business.

Improving Customer Service

Introduction:

Customer service is a critical aspect of any business, including a coffee vending machine business. Happy customers lead to repeat business and positive word of mouth, while poor customer service can quickly damage a company's reputation. In this chapter, we will look at ways to improve customer service and enhance the overall experience for customers.

Listening to customer feedback:

One of the best ways to improve customer service is to listen to customer feedback. This feedback can come from various sources, including customer reviews, surveys, and personal interactions. It's important to take customer feedback seriously, respond to it promptly, and use it to make meaningful improvements to the business.

Providing prompt and efficient service:

Customers expect a quick and seamless experience when using a coffee vending machine. Ensure that the vending machines are well-maintained and fully stocked, and that any issues are resolved as quickly as possible. Offer a clear and concise menu, and make sure the process of purchasing a coffee is straightforward and easy to follow.

Training employees:

Employees are the face of the business, and it's important that they are trained in providing excellent customer service. Teach employees how to handle customer complaints and resolve issues quickly and efficiently. Ensure that employees are knowledgeable about the products and services offered, and encourage them to be friendly and approachable.

Offering value-added services:

Consider offering additional services or products that will enhance the customer experience, such as free Wi-Fi or complementary snacks. These value-added services will help differentiate your business from competitors and make customers more likely to choose your vending machines over others.

Conclusion:

Improving customer service is an ongoing process that requires attention and effort. By listening to customer feedback, providing efficient service, training employees, offering value-added services, and continuously evaluating performance, a coffee vending machine business can provide a positive customer experience and build a loyal customer base.

Establishing a Training Program for Employees

When it comes to running a successful coffee vending machine business, having a team of well-trained employees is crucial. Not only does it ensure that your customers receive the best possible experience, but it also helps streamline operations, minimize errors, and improve overall efficiency.

To achieve this, it's important to establish a comprehensive training program for your employees. This program should cover all aspects of the job, from the basics of operating the vending machine to more advanced skills such as customer service, inventory management, and troubleshooting.

Here are some key steps for establishing an effective training program:

1. Define the objective: Start by defining what you want to achieve with the training program. This could be anything from improving customer service to increasing sales. Having a clear objective in mind will help you create a more focused and effective program.
2. Identify the training needs: Based on your objective, identify the specific skills and knowledge that your employees will need to be successful in their role. This could include machine operation, customer service, inventory management, and more.
3. Develop the content: Based on the training needs, create a comprehensive training manual that covers all the relevant topics. This manual should include step-by-step instructions, images, videos, and other materials that will help your employees understand and apply the information.

4. Choose a delivery method: Consider the best way to deliver the training to your employees. This could be in-person training, online training, or a combination of both. Keep in mind that different employees may have different learning styles, so try to offer a variety of delivery methods to accommodate everyone.
5. Set a timeline: Decide when you want to launch the training program and set a timeline for completion. This will help ensure that your employees are trained in a timely manner and that the program doesn't get pushed to the backburner.
6. Monitor progress: Continuously monitor your employees' progress throughout the training program and make adjustments as needed. This will help you identify areas where employees may be struggling and provide additional support where needed.

By implementing a comprehensive training program for your employees, you'll not only improve their skills and knowledge, but you'll also help ensure the success of your coffee vending machine business. Whether you're just starting out or looking to improve your existing program, these steps can help you establish a training program that works for your team.

Upgrading Coffee Vending Machines

Coffee vending machines play a crucial role in many businesses. As technology evolves, it is important to keep up with the latest advancements in order to stay ahead of the competition and provide the best possible service to customers. In this chapter, we will explore the various ways you can upgrade your coffee vending machines and the benefits of doing so.

Benefits of Upgrading

There are many benefits to upgrading your coffee vending machines. First and foremost, upgrading can help you stay ahead of the competition. The latest coffee vending machines come with improved features and options, such as better brewing systems, larger and more vibrant displays, and increased storage capacity. Upgrading can also help you attract new customers by providing them with a more modern and enjoyable experience.

Another important benefit of upgrading is increased efficiency. Newer coffee vending machines are designed to be more efficient in terms of energy consumption, water usage, and maintenance. This can help reduce costs and increase profitability over the long term. Additionally, many newer coffee vending machines are equipped with sensors and software that can provide real-time data on usage, performance, and maintenance needs, making it easier to manage your business.

Factors to Consider

Before upgrading your coffee vending machines, there are several factors to consider. The first is the cost of the upgrade. Upgrading can be expensive, so it is important to consider your budget and find the best solution for your needs. You should also consider the compatibility of the new machines with your existing systems and infrastructure, as well as the installation process and any required training for employees.

Another important factor to consider is the type of coffee vending machine you are using. There are many different types of coffee vending machines, each with its own strengths and weaknesses. It is important to choose the right type of machine for your needs, taking into account factors such as the volume of coffee you need to dispense, the type of customers you serve, and your budget.

Finally, it is important to consider the features and options you need. Some of the latest coffee vending machines come with features such as adjustable temperature control, customizable menus, and touch screen displays. These features can help improve the customer experience, but they also come at a premium cost.

Choosing the Right Upgrade

When choosing the right upgrade for your coffee vending machines, it is important to consider your needs and budget. You may choose to upgrade your existing machines, or you may choose to purchase new machines entirely. If you are upgrading your existing machines, consider what specific improvements you need, such as a better brewing system, larger storage capacity, or a more user-friendly interface.

If you are purchasing new machines, there are several options to consider. Some of the latest coffee vending machines are equipped with cutting-edge technology such as high-resolution displays, automatic brewing systems, and advanced software for real-time data analysis. Other machines may be designed for specific types of customers, such as those who prefer specialty coffees or those who need a machine that can dispense hot and cold beverages.

Conclusion

Upgrading your coffee vending machines can provide many benefits, including increased efficiency, improved customer experience, and increased profitability. When choosing the right upgrade, it is important to consider your needs, budget, and the type of machine you are using. With the right upgrade, you can stay ahead of the competition and provide the best possible service to your customers.

Building a Company Culture

Introduction: A strong company culture is essential for any business, especially in the coffee vending machine industry. It helps to define the values, beliefs, and behaviors that employees are expected to exhibit. A positive company culture can enhance employee satisfaction, reduce turnover, and improve overall performance.

What is Company Culture? Company culture refers to the personality and character of a business. It is shaped by the company's mission, values, and beliefs, as well as the attitudes and behaviors of its employees. The culture of a business can be expressed through its physical surroundings, communication style, and overall approach to work.

Why is Company Culture Important? A strong company culture can be a competitive advantage. When employees feel connected to the company and its values, they are more likely to be engaged, productive, and committed to the company's success. A positive company culture also helps to attract and retain talent, which is essential for growth and success in the long term.

How to Build a Company Culture:

1. Establish a clear mission and values: Develop a clear mission statement and core values that reflect the company's purpose and goals. These should be communicated to employees and incorporated into all aspects of the business.
2. Foster a positive work environment: Create a work environment that is positive, supportive, and inclusive.

This can include offering flexible schedules, providing opportunities for professional growth and development, and recognizing and rewarding employee contributions.

3. Encourage open communication: Encourage open and honest communication between employees and management. This can include regular check-ins, town hall meetings, and feedback sessions.
4. Promote teamwork: Encourage collaboration and teamwork among employees. This can include team-building activities, cross-functional projects, and opportunities for employees to work together.
5. Lead by example: Company leaders should embody the company's values and mission in their actions and behaviors. They should be approachable and accessible, and actively seek feedback from employees.
6. Continuously evaluate and improve: Regularly evaluate the company culture and make changes as needed. This can include conducting surveys, seeking feedback from employees, and making changes based on that feedback.

Conclusion: Building a strong company culture is essential for success in the coffee vending machine industry. By establishing clear values and goals, fostering a positive work environment, and promoting teamwork and open communication, you can create a culture that supports employee engagement and performance. Regularly evaluating and improving your company culture will ensure that it remains relevant and effective in supporting your business over time.

Developing a Crisis Management Plan

As a business owner, it's important to be prepared for any crisis that may arise. A well-defined crisis management plan can help you respond effectively to unexpected events and minimize the damage to your business. Here are some key steps to help you develop a crisis management plan for your coffee vending machine business.

1. Identify potential crises

The first step in developing a crisis management plan is to identify the types of crises that your business could potentially face. This could include anything from natural disasters to equipment malfunctions, theft, or cyber attacks. Make a list of all the potential crises that your business could face and prioritize them based on their likelihood and potential impact.

2. Assign roles and responsibilities

Once you have identified potential crises, you need to assign specific roles and responsibilities to your employees. This will help ensure that everyone knows what to do in the event of a crisis. For example, you may want to designate a point person who will be responsible for coordinating the response, a communications manager who will handle media inquiries, and a recovery manager who will lead the effort to get the business back up and running.

3. Develop response procedures

Based on the types of crises you've identified, you need to develop specific response procedures. This could include evacuating the building, shutting down certain systems, or communicating with customers. Make sure your procedures are clear, concise, and easy to follow. You should also conduct regular training sessions to ensure that all employees know how to respond in the event of a crisis.

4. Establish a communication plan

Effective communication is key during a crisis. You need to have a plan in place for communicating with employees, customers, suppliers, and other stakeholders. This should include contact information for key personnel, a protocol for communicating important updates, and a plan for using social media and other digital channels to get the word out.

5. Review and update your plan regularly

Finally, it's important to regularly review and update your crisis management plan. This will help ensure that it remains relevant and effective, and that you're prepared for any new types of crises that may arise. You should also conduct regular drills and simulations to test your response procedures and make any necessary adjustments.

In conclusion, a well-defined crisis management plan is a critical component of any successful business. By following the steps outlined above, you can ensure that your coffee vending machine business is prepared to respond effectively to any crisis that may arise.

Managing Risks and Challenges in a Coffee Vending Machine Business

Starting and running a coffee vending machine business can be exciting, but it also comes with a set of challenges and risks. As an entrepreneur, it is important to anticipate and prepare for potential obstacles that may arise. This chapter will help you understand how to manage risks and overcome challenges in your business.

1. Market competition One of the biggest challenges that you may face is market competition. With the increasing popularity of coffee vending machines, the number of competitors in the market has also increased. To stay ahead of the competition, it is important to offer unique and high-quality coffee blends, exceptional customer service, and competitive pricing.
2. Economic downturns The economy can be volatile, and economic downturns can affect the demand for coffee vending machines. To prepare for this, it is important to have a robust financial plan and a diverse customer base. This will help ensure that your business remains profitable, even during tough economic times.
3. Changes in customer preferences Customers' preferences and tastes can change over time, so it is important to stay up-to-date with industry trends and continuously offer new and innovative coffee blends. Keeping an open line of communication with your customers can also help you understand their evolving needs and preferences.

4. Machine breakdowns and maintenance Coffee vending machines require regular maintenance to ensure they are in good working condition. Machine breakdowns can lead to customer dissatisfaction and lost revenue. To minimize the impact of machine breakdowns, it is important to invest in high-quality machines and have a regular maintenance schedule in place.

5. Employee turnover Employee turnover can be a challenge for any business, and it can be especially challenging in the coffee vending machine industry. To mitigate this risk, it is important to have a robust employee training program, offer competitive compensation and benefits packages, and foster a positive work environment.

6. Regulatory compliance The coffee vending machine industry is regulated by government agencies, and it is important to understand and comply with all relevant regulations. Failure to comply with regulations can result in fines, legal action, and damage to your reputation.

In conclusion, managing risks and challenges in a coffee vending machine business requires careful planning and preparation. By anticipating potential obstacles, you can develop strategies to minimize their impact and ensure the success of your business.

Staying Current with Industry News

As a coffee vending machine business owner, it is important to stay informed and up-to-date on the latest industry news and trends. Not only will this help you stay ahead of the competition, but it will also ensure that you are making informed decisions that will benefit your business.

Here are some tips for staying current with industry news:

1. Follow industry publications and websites: Keep yourself updated by subscribing to industry-specific publications and websites. This will give you an insight into the latest trends and happenings in the coffee vending machine industry.
2. Attend trade shows and conferences: Trade shows and conferences provide an excellent opportunity to network with industry professionals and gain insights into the latest advancements and trends in the industry.
3. Connect with other industry professionals: Joining industry organizations and attending events can help you build a network of professionals who can provide valuable information and insights.
4. Follow industry leaders on social media: Industry leaders often share their thoughts and insights on social media, so following them can give you a deeper understanding of the industry.
5. Keep an eye on your competition: Keep track of what your competitors are doing and what changes they are making. This will give you an idea of the industry trends and help you stay ahead of the game.

By staying current with industry news, you will have a better understanding of the industry and be able to make informed decisions that will benefit your coffee vending machine business. Remember, staying up-to-date is crucial to the success of your business.

In conclusion, staying current with industry news is an important aspect of running a successful coffee vending machine business. By following the tips mentioned above, you can stay informed and stay ahead of the competition. So, take the time to stay informed and invest in your business today!

Offering Additional Products and Services

As the owner of a coffee vending machine business, you may be looking for ways to grow and expand your offerings. One way to do this is by offering additional products and services to your customers. This not only helps to increase your revenue, but it can also help to build customer loyalty and establish your business as a one-stop-shop for all things coffee-related.

Here are a few suggestions for additional products and services you can offer:

1. Pastries and Snacks - Offer a selection of pastries and snacks to go along with your coffee. You can include items like muffins, croissants, and breakfast bars. This is a great way to cater to customers who may be looking for a quick breakfast on-the-go.
2. Teas and Hot Cocoa - Offer a variety of teas and hot cocoa options to cater to customers who may not be coffee drinkers. You can also offer flavored teas and hot cocoa for those who want a sweeter option.
3. Cold Beverages - Offer a selection of cold beverages like iced coffee, cold brew, and flavored iced teas. This is a great way to cater to customers who may be looking for a refreshing drink during the hot months.
4. Coffee Accessories - Offer coffee accessories like reusable cups, travel mugs, and coffee stirrers. This is a great way to make additional revenue while also promoting sustainability.
5. Coffee Subscriptions - Offer coffee subscriptions where customers can receive a monthly delivery of coffee beans or K-Cups directly to their door. This is a great

way to build customer loyalty and ensure a steady stream of income.

6. Specialty Coffees - Offer a selection of specialty coffees like espresso, cappuccino, and lattes. You can also offer flavored syrups and toppings to make these drinks even more appealing.

When adding additional products and services to your offerings, it's important to consider the cost and the demand for these items. Make sure to research and evaluate the market to determine what will be successful for your business. Additionally, make sure to keep your vending machines well-stocked and regularly maintained to ensure the quality of your products and services.

By offering additional products and services, you can diversify your business and increase your revenue. This can also help to establish your business as a leader in the coffee vending machine industry and set you apart from your competition. With the right planning and execution, offering additional products and services can be a valuable addition to your business.

Establishing a Presence on Social Media

In today's digital age, having a strong online presence is crucial for businesses of all sizes and industries. Social media platforms such as Facebook, Instagram, and Twitter provide businesses with a powerful tool for reaching out to potential customers, building brand awareness, and promoting their products and services. Here are some tips for establishing a strong and effective social media presence for your coffee vending machine business:

1. Choose the right platforms: Not all social media platforms are created equal, so it's important to choose the ones that are most relevant to your business. If your target audience is primarily on Instagram, then it makes sense to focus your efforts there. On the other hand, if your target audience is more active on Twitter, then that platform might be a better fit.
2. Create a consistent brand image: Across all platforms, make sure that your brand image is consistent. This includes using the same logo, colors, and tone of voice. This helps to build recognition and trust with your followers.
3. Engage with your followers: Social media is all about two-way communication. Encourage followers to engage with your posts by asking questions, responding to comments, and sharing user-generated content.
4. Share valuable content: Share interesting, informative, and relevant content with your followers. This could include behind-the-scenes stories, promotions, and industry news.

5. Utilize paid advertising: Paid advertising on social media platforms can help you reach a wider audience, including people who may not be following your pages yet. Utilize the targeting options offered by the platforms to ensure your ads reach the right people.
6. Keep track of metrics: Use the built-in analytics tools offered by social media platforms to track engagement, reach, and conversions. This information can help you identify which posts are performing well and adjust your strategy accordingly.
7. Stay active and up-to-date: Social media platforms are constantly changing, so it's important to stay current with industry news and trends. This will help you stay relevant and engaged with your followers.

By following these tips, you can establish a strong and effective social media presence that helps you connect with potential customers, build brand awareness, and promote your coffee vending machine business.

Building Relationships with Customers

Running a successful coffee vending machine business is not just about providing high-quality coffee and supplies, it's also about building strong, long-lasting relationships with your customers. By creating a warm and inviting atmosphere and offering personalized service, you can establish yourself as a trusted and reliable provider of coffee, which can help to build customer loyalty and increase repeat business.

Here are some tips for building relationships with your customers:

1. Get to know your customers: Make an effort to learn about your customers, their interests, and their preferences. This can be as simple as asking their name and starting a conversation or using customer data to tailor your offerings to their individual tastes.
2. Offer exceptional customer service: Provide a welcoming and supportive environment and make sure that every customer feels valued. Offer help with any questions they may have, and be willing to go the extra mile to make their experience with your business as positive as possible.
3. Show appreciation: Thank your customers for their business and show your appreciation in small ways, such as offering them a complimentary coffee or providing them with exclusive promotions and discounts.
4. Foster a sense of community: Encourage customers to engage with each other and with your business by hosting events, such as coffee tastings, or by creating a

loyalty program that rewards customers for their repeat business.

5. Respond to feedback: Listen to your customers and take their feedback into consideration. Whether it's a compliment or a complaint, use this information to improve your offerings and make changes that better meet their needs.

6. Stay in touch: Keep your customers informed about your business by sending out regular newsletters, or by using social media to share updates and special promotions.

By building strong relationships with your customers, you can create a loyal customer base that will help to ensure the continued success of your coffee vending machine business. So, be friendly, be responsive, and be willing to go the extra mile to make your customers feel valued. With these strategies in place, you can help to grow your business and achieve your goals.

Preparing for Growth and Success

Starting and growing a business can be a rewarding and challenging experience. One of the keys to success is preparing for growth and success. This chapter will provide you with some tips and strategies to help you achieve your goals.

1. Define your goals and vision

Before you start preparing for growth and success, it's important to define what success means to you. Ask yourself what you want to achieve with your business, what your vision for the future is, and what you hope to accomplish in the short and long term. This will help you focus your efforts and set priorities.

2. Create a solid business plan

A solid business plan is a roadmap for your business that outlines your goals, strategies, and the steps you need to take to achieve them. Your business plan should also include financial projections, including revenue and expense estimates, and a marketing plan that outlines how you plan to reach your target market.

3. Stay focused on your goals

It's easy to get sidetracked by unexpected challenges and opportunities, but staying focused on your goals is critical to success. Make sure you're always working towards your long-term vision and don't let short-term distractions divert you from your path.

4. Build a strong team

A strong team is essential for success. Make sure you have the right people in place who are skilled, knowledgeable, and committed to your vision. Consider hiring employees or partnering with others who can bring expertise and experience to your business.

5. Invest in marketing and advertising

Marketing and advertising are essential to building brand awareness and reaching your target market. Invest in these efforts to help increase your visibility and reach potential customers.

6. Stay up-to-date with industry trends and developments

The business world is constantly changing, so it's important to stay informed about industry trends and developments. Stay up-to-date by attending conferences, networking with other business owners, and reading relevant articles and books.

7. Continuously evaluate your performance

To prepare for growth and success, you need to continuously evaluate your performance and make changes as needed. Regularly review your financial statements, customer feedback, and marketing results to identify areas for improvement.

8. Celebrate your successes

Finally, don't forget to celebrate your successes along the way. Acknowledge the hard work and achievements of yourself and your team, and enjoy the journey.

In conclusion, preparing for growth and success requires focus, commitment, and hard work. By following these tips and strategies, you can set yourself and your business up for long-term success.

Here's a bonus chapter on "Staying Motivated and Positive":

Starting and running a successful business can be challenging, but it is also a rewarding experience. It is important to stay motivated and maintain a positive outlook, even during tough times. Here are some tips for staying motivated and positive:

1. Set achievable goals: Setting achievable goals for your business can help you stay focused and motivated. Be realistic about what you can achieve, and celebrate your accomplishments along the way.
2. Surround yourself with supportive people: Surrounding yourself with positive and supportive people can make a big difference. Find a support group of other business owners or a mentor who can offer advice and encouragement.
3. Take care of yourself: Taking care of your physical and mental health is important for maintaining a positive outlook. Exercise regularly, eat well, and get enough sleep.
4. Stay organized: Staying organized can help you prioritize tasks and avoid becoming overwhelmed. Use tools such as calendars, to-do lists, and task

management software to help keep track of your responsibilities.

5. Celebrate successes: Celebrating your successes, no matter how small, can help you stay motivated and positive. Take time to reflect on what you have accomplished and what you are proud of.

6. Stay adaptable: The business world is constantly changing, and it is important to stay adaptable and open to new ideas. Be willing to change your strategies and approaches as necessary.

7. Stay persistent: Persistence is key to success. Don't give up when faced with obstacles or challenges. Instead, find ways to overcome them and continue working towards your goals.

Remember, success takes time and hard work. Stay motivated and positive, and you will achieve the success you are looking for.

We hope this book has been helpful in your journey to building and growing your business. All the best wishes for your success!

Congratulations on reaching the end of this book! You have learned about various strategies and techniques to help you achieve success in your business. The journey to success is not always easy, but with the knowledge and tools you have acquired, you are well equipped to tackle the challenges that come your way.

We hope this book has provided you with valuable insights and helpful tips that you can put into practice as you continue to grow and develop your business. Remember, success is a journey, not a destination, and the key to success is to always keep learning, growing and adapting to the changing business environment.

Wishing you all the best and success in your future endeavors. Keep pushing forward, stay focused and stay motivated. The world is your oyster!

9 798887 597503 7